# SEASONS OF THE MIND

Edited by

Heather Killingray

First published in Great Britain in 1999 by
ANCHOR BOOKS
1-2 Wainman Road, Woodston,
Peterborough, PE2 7BU
Telephone (01733) 230761

All Rights Reserved

*Copyright Contributors 1999*

HB ISBN 1 85930 618 7
SB ISBN 1 85930 613 6

# *FOREWORD*

Anchor Books is a small press, established in 1992, with the aim of promoting readable poetry to as wide an audience as possible.

We hope to establish an outlet for writers of poetry who may have struggled to see their work in print.

The poems presented here have been selected from many entries. Editing proved to be a difficult task and as the Editor, the final selection was mine.

I trust this selection will delight and please the authors and all those who enjoy reading poetry.

Heather Killingray
Editor

# CONTENTS

|  |  |  |
|---|---|---|
| And Ever Give Us Cause | Pam S Quigley | 1 |
| Regression | Amanda-Lee Manning | 2 |
| The Great Paganino | Antonio Martorelli | 4 |
| Infants | Robert Catlin | 5 |
| Does Age Matter? | Mary Hoyle | 6 |
| Too Young To Know | Joanne Davison | 7 |
| Drugs | Janet Bowen | 8 |
| Short And Sharp | M Haselden | 9 |
| Does Age Matter? | Gary Gibbs | 10 |
| Backward March | Barbara Sherlow | 11 |
| To The Parent | Henry J Green | 12 |
| Save Our World | Margaret Webb | 14 |
| Police Plight | Janet Boulton | 16 |
| Spare The Rod | Paul Gold | 17 |
| Stress | Helen Jones | 18 |
| Does Age Matter? | Helena Edwards-Bishop | 19 |
| Millennium Families | Peggy Cummins | 20 |
| Does Age Matter | B Brown | 21 |
| A Royalist | Margaret Andrews | 22 |
| Blame Us All | Jackie Coman | 24 |
| Democracy | Lachlan Taylor | 25 |
| Fond Memories Of Diana, Princesss . . . . | Brian Harris | 26 |
| Boudicca | Kim Montia | 27 |
| The Age Of Society | Helen Steel | 28 |
| Who's To Blame? | Dorothy Aplin | 30 |
| The Evidence | Val Barton | 31 |
| What's War For? | Colin Allsop | 32 |
| Leave 'Em Alone! | Di Bagshawe | 33 |
| Our Queen Mother | Margaret Jackson | 34 |
| Royalty Is Fine! | Marjorie Cowan | 35 |
| Too Great The Divide | Elizabeth Read | 36 |
| Diana | Dawn Leslie | 38 |
| A Cry For Help | Paul A Cushen | 39 |
| Our Gracious Queen | Gwen Haines | 40 |

| | | |
|---|---|---|
| Spotlight | P Morrill | 41 |
| Our Royals | B D S Leith | 42 |
| The Royals | Leonard T Coleman | 43 |
| The Royals | Joan Patrickson | 44 |
| The Royals | Marion D Harris | 45 |
| HRH | Fiona Bower | 46 |
| The Royals | Ken Mills | 47 |
| HRH Or Lack Of | Albert H Williams | 48 |
| The Royals | Dorothy Campbell | 50 |
| Diana . . . | J M Service | 51 |
| Regal Rundown | Susan Melville | 52 |
| 'Scandal?' Never! | Susan Askew | 53 |
| Death Of A Princess | Beverley Christian | 54 |
| The Royals | Hilary Jill Robson | 55 |
| Royalty Personified | Jim Wilson | 56 |
| Right Royal | Jane Uff | 58 |
| Thank You Ma'am For Forty Years | Wenn The Penn | 59 |
| The Royals - Only Human After All | Cathy Mearman | 60 |
| Our Royal Family | D Naylor | 61 |
| Who Asked Us? | P J Gassner | 62 |
| This Grief I Bear | Denise Shaw | 63 |
| Royal Delight | L Beardsley | 64 |
| The Royal Family | Linda Brown | 65 |
| The Royals | Lorraine Saunders | 66 |
| Queen And Country | Andrew Darkin | 67 |
| Royal | Enid Gill | 68 |
| Noel | Albert Usher | 69 |
| Try To Be Friendly | Willaim Howarth | 70 |
| Untitled | P Allen | 71 |
| Summertime Gone Wrong | Gillian Connors | 72 |
| Spring | Marie Barker | 73 |
| Healing Hands | Karen Caldwell | 74 |
| Moving On (With God) | Hilary I Jones | 75 |
| Vandals | Clive W Macdonald | 76 |
| Does Age Matter | Allan Lambert | 77 |
| This World | E B Holcombe | 78 |

| | | |
|---|---|---|
| The Victim | Dennis N Davies | 79 |
| Does Age Matter? | J L Thorne | 80 |
| Return To Moral Values | Susan Mullinger | 81 |
| Ageless | M C Lawrence | 82 |
| Freedom? | Ray Baker | 83 |
| Children Of Delinquency | Carl A Dignan | 84 |
| Questions | Trevor Vincent | 85 |
| Where The Fault Lies | Thomas C Ryemarsh | 86 |
| Not A Bit | Vivienne Doncaster | 87 |
| Mystery Of Murder | Kathleen Speed | 88 |
| Infected Youth A Criminal Gene | Samantha Mitchell | 89 |
| And So To Bed | Carrington Lee | 90 |
| Apology | Roy Brown | 91 |
| Second Wind | Roy Turke | 92 |
| Does Age Matter? | Joan Scowcroft | 93 |
| Down | J R Wiseman | 94 |
| Mother Love | S T Jennings | 95 |
| The Aged And Our Young | Phoebe J Laing | 96 |
| Hand It To Me On A Plate | Maureen Albert | 97 |
| Time For Spring | Margaret Upson | 98 |
| The Swaying Rowan Tree | Pearl Mansell | 99 |
| An Everlasting Spring Day | Malaka Chowdhury | 100 |
| Spring | Fatima Jamshad | 101 |
| Kaleidoscope | Ian Caughey | 102 |
| Autumn Leaves | Michael A Moore | 103 |
| The Changing Seasons | Lorna June burdon | 104 |
| Autumn Days | Elwynne | 105 |
| Autumn | B Wilson | 106 |
| Autumn Leaves | S Buckingham | 107 |
| Winter Cheer | Jessica Street | 108 |
| When Wintry Winds Blow | Annemarie Poole | 109 |
| Autumn Whispers | Grace Wade | 110 |
| Autumn Falls | Peggy Keogh | 111 |
| Winter | J-C Chandenier | 112 |
| Changing Seasons | Sonia Richards | 113 |
| A Whole Year | Susan J MacDonald | 114 |
| Nature's Diary | R R Shepherd | 115 |

| | | |
|---|---|---|
| Springtime | Sheila M Tebbutt | 116 |
| The Rose Tree That Grew Again | Irene Dodd | 117 |
| Autumn Prayer | David Rhine | 118 |
| Seasons Change | Sylvia Connor | 119 |

## AND EVER GIVE US CAUSE

Hello Queen,

I know you have been having a tough time lately with the so-called experts. Trying to make you something like the rest of us. You paying tax and everything. I know you do now - and thanks very much - but I sometimes wonder what they do with your money. I've never noticed anything different since you started paying. I can't see the point of making you like the rest of us. I mean, I may as well look up to Mrs Battersby next door if you Royals start being like us. When I was little, in the Brownies, I promised to do my duty to God and the Queen - see what I mean? Another thing, about the family, well, what I say is - you bring the kids up best you can - after that - it's up to them. Besides, we only get told what they want us to know. How do we know what's the truth? Trouble is you get stuck into an image. Now me - where I live, we're supposed to eat scouse every day and talk through our adenoids. Not far from here they reckon they breed ferrets and wear flat caps - All the time. Just one thing - do us a favour and stop that Charles from shooting all the little furry things and the poor birds. Apart from that, most of my life you've been
The one upon the throne. Keep going Queen.

Best wishes, your mostly obedient servant.

*Pam S Quigley*

## REGRESSION

The youth of today have mostly had a raw deal, but do not have the
Strength of character for self improvement or betterment.
The family unit as we once knew it, has completely broken down,
Gone are the days when grandparents were able to step in at a moment's
Notice, thus saving the youngsters from street roaming and offering a
Loving environment.
Both parents work full-time as needs must nowadays, to keep the
Standard of living, they have become accustomed to, to buy that new
Video, have a holiday or two!
The children fend for themselves, rushing to McDonald's after school,
With the fiver mum gave him that morning, maybe he'll buy a burger,
Maybe not.
Then street walking with his mates, bored, frustrated looking for
Excitement, he meets new friends, bad influences, he samples his first
Drug, washed down with alcohol, and smoking pot, he is only twelve
Years old.
Unused to the sensation, or the messages being sent to his brain,
He reacts unpredictably, violent, causing mayhem to anything in his
Path.
Should he survive his first trip, he may wake up in police custody,
Whilst his parents are being traced, their total lack of understanding,
And total hostility towards the police, can only be excused,
Because they don't know any better, probably once having been down
The same road, without parental control and unable to even imagine
What TLC is or was.
They leave with their off-spring swearing and cursing at the authority,
Who arrested their *'Darlin Kevin',* when they themselves hardly see
Him, years later, too many videos and drugs, have moulded *Kevin* into
A slob.
He expects to walk into a job because of his arrogance and pushy
Approach, or he can go on the dole like his brothers and uncles.
An uncouth yob, who cannot even complete an application form due
To illiteracy.

The negative responses cause resentment and anger which triggers a
Volatile streak, the dole queues increase, some have never worked at all
Since leaving school, grudgingly stating that *'No one wants them, so
They'll never work!'*
They are right of course, no one wants trouble, or inexperienced
Employees, but who pays for lunch at the pub, the betting shop in the
Afternoon, *who is to blame?*

***Amanda-Lea Manning***

## THE GREAT PAGANINO

He was a genius from the beginning, he had a special gift of hearing music in the air. He could not play the violin but the people pushed him to play. In desperation he started to play and soon he broke most of the cords or strings. The people started to laugh at him. He started to play and he was wonderful and all asked him to repeat it but he could not because he did not know how and he said to the people Paganino do not repeat himself and from that day he became the only master and the first genius of the violin. In reality he did not know anything of music or play the violin, but played the most difficult piece of music with one string. He had his day of magic. Later in his life he worked very hard to master the violin and after that he was the supreme master of the world. Nobody could play like him not before or after his death. He was born a genius and he died virtuous. Paganino was and still is the only man to play the violin on one string only. Lucky for him, I could not play anything.

*Antonio Martorelli*

# INFANTS

We were on a nature outing
Class 1 with old Mrs Knight
And young Bobby Bruce
Found instead of his juice
A bottle of whisky
His dad won at bingo last night.
We all had a sup
From an old plastic cup
And thought it a bit of all right.
The kids all fell about laughin'
A laughin' fit to bust
And little Tommy Biddle
Had a quiet little piddle
In the corner in a heap of old dust.
Little Fanny Vickers
Wet her flannel knickers
And happy Winnie Martin
Ended up by fartin'
And we all fell about laughin' ag'in.

*Robert Catlin*

## DOES AGE MATTER?

A kinder boy you could not meet
But earth and stars don't touch his feet.
When alcohol his lips do taste
The pints they down with so much haste.
His life is thro' at 25 years
I stand and watch with many tears.
The trouble increases day to day
His habit 'I know' will stay.
*No* not prison jail he cries again
I want to stop and end this pain.
He needs some help maybe someone
Who hears his cries and comes along.
To cure his head of all he ails
Please God help him, no more jails!
Age to me does matter Lord
I know he's always giving his word
To behave and not commit a crime
But he's so young to do his time -
When others should be there to help him
They never are so he will sin -

A caring onlooker I will be
Please God, help him to be free.

*Mary Hoyle*

## TOO YOUNG TO KNOW

Another brick crashed through the door
The boys rush in to steal once more
You'd think they'd be too young to know
They're not much more than ten or so.

I often think of all this crime
And think they all should do the time
It doesn't matter what their age
They too should be locked in a cage.

You hear the children killing others
Sometimes fathers, sometimes mothers
Because they're young, they set them free
I'd be in prison if it were me.

It shouldn't matter how old they are
If they rob, murder or steal a car
If they were older they would pay
They'd be locked up by noon today.

The children say they've nothing to do
So they pray on people like me and you
They rob our homes and steal our cars
Get in pubs and drink in bars.

Some are obnoxious, crude and loud
Others get in with the wrong crowd
Whatever the circumstances of who's to blame
They should go to prison all the same.

*Joanne Davison*

## DRUGS

The bane of our society, destroying lives so young,
Respect for themselves and others, have long since been o'er run.
Pushers and dealers are to blame, the barons unconcerned;
They live their lives in luxury, their consciences unturned.

But God will have retribution; one day all will be judged,
So listen now you poor addicts, seek help from Him above.
He's the only one who'll help you, through those who serveth Him,
Cast off all worldly pleasures and He'll cleanse your life from sin.

*Janet Bowen*

## SHORT AND SHARP

Security, few like, some dread,
But solitude breeds rats in head,
And be it that there's cut-throats there,
With commune their experience share.
Not two pence would I give for hope
Of building up the brain to cope
With better things on men's release
From prison cells held by police.
It costs a mint to keep them there,
And that the country cannot bear.

Of yore the stocks were proved a cure,
Now of course they'd cause uproar.
How about they're taken high,
To rooftops open to the sky.
In prison garb they're made to stand,
Jeered at from the streets below,
With spectacle for all to see,
Despicable they're made to be.
Shame digs deeper than can tell,
For repetition of such hell.

*M Haselden*

## DOES AGE MATTER?

Come and join the Genocide Club
Young people apply for this position
As long as you own a knife and gun
It's free admission
The killers of Steven Lawrence
I saw those stoic eyes, their confident position
It made me angry with their
Lack of contrition.
What is happening to our schools, when
In a 15 year old's pocket, lies a knife
And another Lawrence, a benign teacher
Had to play cruelly with his life?
Kids must know home is for discipline
And school is to educate
If a young child hasn't any
Of that
Saving from crime could be
Too late.

*Gary Gibbs*

## BACKWARD MARCH

Banners and flags hoisted
Minds, hearts, stiff as starch
Adults of the world
Take the backward march.

Undermined are people
In this way and that
As we try undo
Government's stupid chat.

For children have grown up
Knowing they can do
Anything they want
With punishment's taboo.

And so they've carried on
Mugging, thugging, theft
That backward march - of
Discipline they're bereft.

Oh - does age matter - no
But too late - teenagers
Dam - damned they, now,
Yes, put them in cages.

The army too is good
For these young cowards
A government did
Make these young empowered.

Conservative's Michael Howard
Sank the children of the 70s/80s/90s
Through refusing necessary
Discipline on them.
He still carries on smugly smiling!

*Barbara Sherlow*

## TO THE PARENT

It's the way you bring 'em up that counts
Not the money that you spend;
Nor coddling to spoil the child
So they on you depend.

It's the way you hold the reins in check
And cuff when they abuse,
The road that's right, the one to point
So it, they later choose.

Correcting them may give you pain
When they turn on the tears,
Be firm and fair, unruffled
Until the trauma clears.

All children know how far to go
But will overstep the line,
It's up to parents how they turn
Make sure they turn out fine.

It's the way you bring 'em up, indeed
By example and direction;
By advice and help, when needed
For waywardness correction.

If you let 'em wander on the street
Just because they're in the way,
Don't have 'em in the first place
Enjoy your empty day.

It's the way you bring 'em up that counts
A great commitment venture,
Half measures bring you no reward
Just volunteered indenture.

Your guardianship through tender years
To keep the straight and narrow;
To strike the target centre
With well-aimed moral arrow.

Then your reward for given love
A son or loving daughter bright,
To comfort in your twilight years
In dark despair your light.

Neglect the guides of common sense
And do so to your cost,
Of peace of mind in later times
When unit ties are lost.

It's the way you bring 'em up that counts
For louts, their heartless actions,
Were yours to mould to right or wrong
To God's or devil's factions.

***Henry J Green***

## SAVE OUR WORLD

*Enter* a world whose beauty now forgotten, a world of destruction, a world dying
*Gone* the unification and infusion needed for a world worth saving.
*Enter* a world of irrational thoughts and behaviour
*Gone* is the love, peace, harmony and honour.
*Enter* a world of disobedience and untamed tempers
*Gone* is the caring, sharing, support and favours.
*Enter* a world of illiteracy, doomed for failures
*Gone* is the interest and respect for our superiors.
*Enter* a world of illegitimacy and unaccountable fear
*Gone* are the moral values that once held dear.
*Enter* a world of violence, destruction and murders
*Gone* is our security and the reason for safety in numbers.
*Enter* a world of theft, mugging, burglary and forced entries
*Gone* the freedom to own valuables, our delightful commodities.
*Enter* a world of youth whose guidance is not pursued
*Gone* our patience when all that appears is apparent bad news.
*Enter* a world of people whose clear eyed views are constantly rejected
*Gone* is our desire to help in order to keep our integrity protected.
*Enter* a world forced into confusion, atrocities, struggle and strife
*Gone* our ability to look to another source to improve our life.
*Enter* a world with a saviour a trust in whom we so desperately need
*Gone* will be resentment and ridicule replaced with the ability to water God's seed.
*Enter* a world blinded by famine, war, destruction and earthquake
*Gone* the need to accept responsibility for the world, our most valuable stake.

*Enter* a world of supremacy who ignores the call of justice
*Gone* the staying power to remain in the kingdom under God's auspice.
*Enter* a world dying, searching, crying and yearning to be saved
*Gone* should be our denial and pre-emption all upon God's shoulders can be laid.
*Enter* a world of wholeness, a promise of healing by God's powerful source
*Gone* will be the guilt of our own doing - forgiven by God, of course.

**Margaret Webb**

## POLICE PLIGHT

Oh! what a night it's been,
Indeed it's been a hectic night.
Our first response was to the scene
Where several drunks were having a fight.
As we arrived the men looked mean,
Exhausted, the punches lost their might,
To continue the fight they were not keen,
With blood covered face, one was a sight.

Then a call to a respectable house,
The owners a pleasant evening had spent,
With some friends, while man, not mouse,
Had broken in, to the bedroom he went,
Stole treasured jewellery, the unkind louse.
The owner despaired, her heart was rent,
Feelings of anguish and sorrow did arouse.
Why don't burglars stop and repent?

The victims head, the aggressor slugs,
Snatches a bag, escapes like an eel.
Is it to support a habit of drugs,
That makes a person want to steal?
I suppose it makes them feel smug,
When they do not care how others feel.
I doubt if they would feel so smug,
If they were dealt this unfair deal.

*Janet Boulton*

## SPARE THE ROD

What can we do, about our *unruly children?*
Whose greatest forte - is destruction - and playing the fool,
And given the slightest opportunity
Would not hesitate - about burning down the school.

And what can we do, about those *unruly parents?*
Storming into classrooms - threatening *teacher* with a *black eye,*
Whilst young *Johnny Jones* - sits smirking behind his desk
To his *mum and dad* - he is *their* apple pie.

Of course - we could follow the example of *Singapore*
Where their *laws,* make a lot of common sense
Where *litter droppers* of any age - are heavily fined
Where to *contaminate* the *public highway* - is an offence.

Where - *unruly behaviour* - is considered to be a *serious crime*
For any young person - above the age of twelve,
Where a *term of imprisonment,* is considered to be the *norm*
In *Singapore, teenagers* have learnt to behave themselves.

Today in *Britain, wrong-doers* are becoming younger and younger
For a *very serious crime,* it's high time they stood in the *dock,*
To await sentence - to a selected *juvenile prison*
If only for a week - *incarcerated* - for a *short, sharp, shock.*

For far *too long* - we have become a nation of *softies*
*Mollycoddling* our *children* - against the cold world outside,
Nevertheless - what with *teacher bashing - rowdyism -* and *drug abuse*
It's high time we parents stopped swimming against the tide.

**Paul Gold**

## STRESS

A man in stature
But a child in age
Yet who should warrant for all this rage?
Young years are for learning
To become so great
Not like mentors who intimidate
So teach young waywards from
Early age that society cannot
Tolerate this rage
Yes for these babes, their parents
Should also go
For as the prophets preach
Thou shall reap what thou
Shall sow.

***Helen Jones***

## DOES AGE MATTER?

But he's so young!
They say. What's he doing this time of night on the town?
Where are his parents? Doesn't he have a home?
Little tearaway! Delinquent, scum of the earth, disgusting!
Blame the parents! They moan.
What for? They're helpless; hands hog-tied
By threats from social bureaucrats - supposed benevolent
Guardians of the law. Yes, home discipline has died.
Dare to smack or clip him around the ear
And you could soon be living in fear.
Legal eagles would soon be hard on your heels
With charges of assault and battery, child abuse.
Justice for them with benevolence turning the wheels.
Fancy doing time in a cell for his sake?
Then just turn a blind eye and a deaf ear or that could be your mistake.
He's just pinched some CDs from that record store
Told the angry manager 'You can't touch me mate - I'm under aged and that's the score.'
Saw one just the other day, mugging an old lady
Beat her up so badly using her own brolly.
Seemed pleased with himself; in fact, quite jolly.
Detention centres separate from senior misfits.
Undisclosed identities - a shielded life of mystery;
Lenient penalties for savage crimes such as rape, mugging, violence
and murder.
Change tactics we say! Deal with them accordingly -
Regardless of their age.
Expose their faces on the telly - print their crimes on stick-on badges
For all to see.
Let them clean trenches, drains and garbage until their hands are raw.
Sober meaningful deeds for such deviants of the law.

*Helena Edwards-Bishop*

## MILLENNIUM FAMILIES

One mum, one dad,
Little money, tired love,
But, a balance to our lives
Before they went above!

Still, one mum, one dad,
Carry on the job,
More money, too much love,
Not fussy who they rob:

Four mums, four dads,
Working all the hours,
Confused children, have no rules
Just weeds, amongst the flowers:

In my long life,
I've seen so many changes,
The Millennium is almost here,
Is there to be danger?

***Peggy Cummins***

## DOES AGE MATTER

Does age matter? Yes my friend
It is with us until the very end
Normally we travel through
Honest, loving and always true.

But there are many today I fear
Who will not obey and will not hear
They are vicious and cruel to man and beast
They look for trouble and work the least.

They thieve and wound and sometimes kill
Have they a grudge or are they ill?
They go to court and sometimes get bail
All usually end up in jail.

What is the reason many I'd say
Children are left alone all day
They hate the rich for they are poor
The rich need less, they need more.

Money seems to be the key
What we are or what we will be
Perhaps if we could see their plight
With kindness and help we could put it right.

*B Brown*

## A Royalist

Perhaps I am living in a fantasy land
But I like palaces high and mighty, beautiful and grand.
When Queen Elizabeth was crowned I waved madly from the side of
    the street
I'd walked miles but I wasn't tired although I had sore feet.

I believe the changing of the guards still happens at Buckingham Palace
And still going to see it are undoubtedly Christopher and Alice,
It is now open to the public to view its greatness and splendour inside
And people come to view it from many a land - from far and wide.

The pageantry, pomp and ceremony still grab my heart
They're so far removed from the humble rumbling horse and cart,
The costumed guards in full regalia are quite a sight to see -
Without this where would Great Britain in her red, white and blue
    plumes be?

I admit that I'm a fanatic and collect all the royal artefacts -
I wash them, polish them and display them in my large union jack;
I never miss a television programme about British Royalty
To them I'm devoted - give them my undivided loyalty.

When Queen Elizabeth II became a mother, I celebrated with
    champagne
I could feel true blue blood running through my commoner's truly red
    veins
The dustbins were home to bad newspaper articles written by the gutter
    press
And who presented the Queen Mother with a small posy
When she visited our local hospital? Well, you've guessed!

Today they take polls to decide whether we wish to abolish this
hereditary institution
Criticise their accents - in my day to achieve this we had lessons called
formal elocution.
They are mocked, impersonated, pilloried and so have decided to be
modern in outlook
But I shall always love them in my humdrum life washing, cleaning and
rushing home to cook!

*Margaret Andrews*

### BLAME US ALL

A stern voice or a clip round the ear
Used to instil our children with fear,
That's something now the loyal boys in blue
Are told they no longer can do.

The cane or the slipper once was the rule
Keeping the peace in every school,
Now misconduct and truancy is rife
What a terrible start in a child's life!

Rules have always been tested and tried
Man made laws keep our hands tied,
The leaders are useless, I don't understand
How can we learn with no punishment at hand.

Some parents need teaching, they don't seem to care,
Where are the morals? Just disappeared!
Addicts of pot, sex and booze
From disease and illness their lives they will loose.

Our babies when born are pure of mind
Only learning wrong doing of every kind
From life and it's living from adults and such
Lacking in standards and not enough love.

*Jackie Coman*

## DEMOCRACY

I believe Royalty is a system
   Which no country should ever have
Especially if there is poverty
   And some people have to starve

Taxes paid out to all the Royals
   Could be put to better use
In helping out those people
   With their poverised abuse

When they say we're democratic
   How do Royalty gain selection
When people never voted here
   Surely this needs a correction

Citizens should have a say here
   If they wish a king or queen
Then you could state democracy
   Is working and can be seen

***Lachlan Taylor***

## FOND MEMORIES OF DIANA, PRINCESS OF WALES
## (1961-1997)

Her smile, so bright,
'neath sparkling blue eyes.
Warm greetings, hugs
and gestures keen.
Love and compassion evoking sighs
from the strong,
or faithless their God unseen.

Diana sought-out
and conquered evil all.
Children, too, recognised
her special grace.
Fame and glory disdained them she.
Her sacrifice upheld an angelic face.

She passed our way
and we are proud to have loved her.
She cast a light that made our path easier to tread.
She was sunshine and flowers
and our home echoes to her laughter.
She passes on to life
and leaves us to a world so dead.

*Brian Harris*

## BOUDICCA

Bold and regal, hair of flame
She played the Romans at their game
So quick to lift her sword to fight
Icceni queen 'gainst Caesar's might

Fear was a concept unbeknown
She loved her enemies to groan
On battlefields she taught them all
How they before this queen should fall

Drenched English land with Roman blood
And rubbed their noses in its mud
A leader who could stir men's hearts
Deciding when the battle starts

Boudicca, the warrior queen
That history cannot demean
What modern royal can compare
To the queen with fire for her hair?

*Kim Montia*

# THE AGE OF SOCIETY

'The prison's full!' the judge announced.
With 90 hours community service, out the prisoner flounced!

The children read the headline with glee,
'Your mam's wrong! We can't go to prison, *see!'*
So, thoroughly bored, with youth club closed,
And prison no longer the threat it once posed,
Ripper lead the toughest gang in town,
Soon the school would be burnt down.
A latch-key kid, who'd seen all the video horrors,
(Anything he wants, he just simply borrows!)
He'd never known an orderly life,
*Discipline* only gave him strife.
So now that he was suspended from school,
He planned to show everyone he was no fool.
Into the boiler room he crept,
A fire he set and the flames soon leapt,
The strident alarms began to ring,
From across the road, Ripper watched the whole thing.
The main doors opened and children spilled out.
Ripper laughed, when he heard screams and shouts.
Emergency services were soon on the scene,
Hmm . . . someone trapped inside Ripper did glean.
In went the firemen with BA sets on,
Two steps into the smoke and they were gone.
Thick black plumes spewed out everywhere,
Inside was black, choking, devoid of air.
They brought out the headmaster, who coughed and choked.
Ripper and his gang laughed and joked!
But Ripper's face was soon a cloud,
Suddenly he screamed out loud!
As out of the inferno came firemen with
His mam, all limp. He remembered their tiff.
She'd said she'd stick up for him and sort it out,
He'd screamed and yelled and then flounced out.

No prison, no sentence, no punishment,
Could ever, ever compliment,
The anguish he now felt inside,
He could run away, he'd go and hide!

The judge he did decry the deed,
'Badness runs through Ripper like a parasitic weed!'
He sent him to prison for five long years,
Ripper left the dock in handcuffs and tears.
'You did the crime and you'll pay the price,
What you did, just was not nice!
You could have killed a whole lot more,
Such callous actions I do deplore!
To be so wicked when you're so young,
I wonder what society has done!'
The merits of good discipline the judge he praised,
And of stability in children's younger days.

Society must share some of the blame,
Society must share some of the shame!
To think that we have failed so badly,
That, offenders turn to crime so gladly,
At ever such a tender age. And just when did it become uncool,
To go out weekly to Sunday School?
The moral standards of society have deminished,
The fabric of our society is now finished!

*Helen Steel*

## WHO'S TO BLAME?

Single mothers, absent fathers
Latch-key kids home alone
Giros that don't last as long as they should
Going out stealing - just to buy food
Drinking, smoking, doing drugs
No one cares about the kids
It's no wonder they turn to crime
It's all they've known for a long time

They see mum do it at the supermarket store
Just little things - she goes back again for more
Dad picks pockets to have a puff
Breaks into houses - it's never enough
Kids watching think it must be right
To go out stealing day and night
It's not very long before they're hooked too
'Can't afford that CD? I'll get it for you'

One day they go out to steal and get caught
'Own up sonny - is that the lot?'
End up doing time in a remand home
There they're shown right from wrong
Will they remember when they've gone home
Or is back to the life they've known
Stealing, drinking, doing drugs
It won't be long before they're back facing the judge!

Who's to blame? Why society
They don't really care about you or me
They live in flash houses and drive fancy cars
They probably don't even know who we are
Someone, somewhere has to begin
To investigate why and where crime will end!

*Dorothy Aplin*

## THE EVIDENCE

A mother and I hang my head in shame, our son in the local paper again
And discredited the family name, am I to blame?
Young and bold many lies he told
And towards me his heart had grown cold.
The squad car would come out the door he'd run,
To him it seemed much fun.
As a child he had no fear
And through the years this became clear.
Drug abuse and also a thug,
And if I could change him do you not think I would?

Not the child I once bore
And today he has no respect for the law.
When young, much love and discipline was given
And now a man, a wild life he's living.
The verdict guilty he did plead
And his drug addict no longer could he feed.
The judge sentenced him once again
And in this prison a son of mine is detained.
Within the jail drugs were rife,
That's when he took his own life
And inside no help had been given,
Now he's dead and I am still living,
The same question I ask again,
As a mother, am I to blame?

*Val Barton*

# WHAT'S WAR FOR?

What did you do in the war dad?
I buried my mates and I was sad
Laid their bodies in the mud
Took my gun and drew blood
I had to take another life
Make a widow of some bloke's wife
Marched behind a blooming drum
Gave heartache to your mum
Don't know what it was for
Can't make sense of going to war.

What was the war like dad?
A real evil, something bad
All about the death you could smell
Guns and bombs and the blooming shells
Bodies laying all around
Tried to take a patch of ground
Put bodies in their bags
Gave the dying their last fags
Made love to some French whore
That was my highlight of this war.

*Colin Allsop*

## LEAVE 'EM ALONE!

The paparazzi buzz like a blue bottle fly,
With inventive mind and lenses that pry.
What new scandal can we stir,
Which vague hints to merely 'infer'?
Divorces and scandals are nothing new,
Over the centuries they've had quite a few,
Surely without the Royal capers
What could they find to sell their papers?
But as for the Royals, they can relax,
Not many reigns now end with an axe!
Looking around this chaotic world,
At fresh governmental horrors unfurled,
I personally can think of no worse fate
Than to have to live in a monarchless state.

*Di Bagshawe*

## OUR QUEEN MOTHER

Always radiant with a smile on her face
an elegant lady with so much grace.
She wins the hearts of everyone
her warmth just flows and she's full of fun.
During the war years tragedies were great
courageously she stayed in London to wait
and support the King ever by his side
commitment to duty - energy ne'er did subside.
So very active throughout her life
as Queen, Queen 'Mum', grandmother and wife.
Dogs, horses, fishing and travelling too,
theatres, reading and walking she'll do.
Family gatherings are also a must
a marvellous welcome we honour and trust.
Such a gift of life and touch of gold
does reach your heart no matter how old.
Full of affection that we all love to cheer
when catching a glimpse year after year.
Sharing happiness and comfort every day
giving much of herself in this unique way.
A remarkable person our Queen Mother be
valiant, joyous, devoted to her family.
An inspiration to all this special belle
her kindness and charm a 'magical spell'.

*Margaret Jackson*

## ROYALTY IS FINE!

I've always felt countries with Royalty at head,
Are the most peaceful, less wars and bloodshed!
If the Royalty is democratic, caring, sincere
As our royalty has been for many a year,
Dignified certainly, but with thoughts for rich and poor;
Their encouraging walkabouts, speeches and so much more,
Great sums to charities to help people live,
They have to be pretty moneyed to these so to give,
And to travel to many places far away,
To support them out there, for happier day.
I think some of the young have a chip on shoulder to grind:
'The Royals being so rich, they cannot abide!'
A stupid attitude, I so think.
If they were to go, we would go down the brink!

*Marjorie Cowan*

## TOO GREAT THE DIVIDE

And where's the father? You tell me!
No one to clip his ear you see.

Spare the rod and spoil the child.
Stands to reason he'd turn out wild.

>Mum's at work, old man cleared out.
>All he ever did was shout.

I blame the teachers, no respect.
Social education! What do you expect?

Birch the big louts. Canes in schools,
Beat them 'til they know the rules!

>School's a bore, none of them care.
>What does it matter if I'm not there?

Didn't do me any harm,
Teacher's stick across the palm.

Should get off his bum and find a job.
He's nothing but a lazy sod!

>Nothing to do but draw the dole.
>No jobs, no future, a big black hole.

Lock him up! Throw away the key.
Rotten kids are no use to me.

I fought a war for the likes of him.
What a waste! It's a ruddy sin.

>Easy money to be had on the streets
>Old girls' bags are full of treats.

Bring back National Service, yes!
Two years Boot Camp, nothing less.

Teach him how to use a gun.
I'd make a man of you, my son!

                        So what if I end up in the nick?
                        Back with me mates, I'll learn new tricks.

*Elizabeth Read*

# Diana

There's a member of the Royal family
We all miss so very much
She was the People's Princess
Who had the special touch

She tried to make a difference
To everyone she saw
Even though inside at times
Her own suffering she bore

She showed a heart of kindness
With a touch or smile or word
And for the ill, the weak and humble
She made their voices heard

Diana was the Princess
Who had the special touch
Now in a better place
And who we miss so very much.

**Dawn Leslie**

# A Cry For Help

Imprisoned by the system for trying to make ends meet,
In prison as a juvenile just for stealing a sweet,
We know not what we do, when we are young and unaware,
Maybe a way to attract attention just to see if people care,
Or is it a cry for help that nobody really seems to hear?
Lock them up and lose the key, a parent's biggest fear,
As young offenders age, they grow up learning more and more,
With criminal knowledge twice as mean and bad as time before,
By now they're stealing cars and robbing banks and harder crime,
They're mugging old ladies in the streets, and getting much more time,
The government only starting to listen to the parent's pleas,
Help us find a way so we can set our children free,
Putting them away for petty crime won't solve the mess,
Our children need a challenge and adventure, something new,
What else is left but crime when there's nothing else to do?
If we work hard together we can make the future great,
And act on every 'cry for help' to keep a good, clean slate.

*Paul A Cushen*

## OUR GRACIOUS QUEEN

Our gracious Queen tries to do her best
For all her many tasks she takes
Up early and works late
The red box ever by her side
The country has always been her guide.

She keeps a critical eye
On all that goes on
Her willingness to loyally serve
To travel far, and with the media is at ease
Elizabeth the Second carries on.

On glamorous occasions of state
Our Queen is immaculately
And appropriately dressed, and we should be proud
I've never been a fan, but she
Would be my number one.

Good, courageous, a mother blessed by four
I'm sure she is loved for evermore
Always had the common touch
But of late, her feelings she has shown
And her nice smile is for all to see, very much.

Over the years that she has reigned
Times have dramatically changed
Her family always her main concern, and
Devoutly religious, she has stamped the seal
This country would the poorer be, without the crown.

**Gwen Haines**

## Spotlight

The splendour of the uniforms
Once again, the guard is being changed;
When it's time to remember; the sadness,
The honour of parades.
Our Royals are our England -
We would be nothing without
The horse guards and the pageantry,
The cheering, and the shout;
Three cheers for all their family.
Queen Mother so loyal and proud.
Mistakes have been made,
We all make those, why expect
Them to be what we aint?
The spotlights always shine -
The cameras always flash on the
Faces of friends of the famous, and
Our Royals are surely this.
People come from countries so
Different to our own; fascinated by the
Beauty; the Majesty of our throne.
Change we feel is coming; but
Remember, the ones who promote.
Change must be for the good of all,
The rich, and us the folk.

*P Morrill*

## OUR ROYALS

For o'er a thousand years,
The Royal Standard has flown,
Over our domain,
And our Queen has shown,
Her loyalty to her throne,
Through all the years,
Through peace, through war,
Through tears,
She has travelled the globe,
For Britain's welfare,
Faithful and loyal and sincere,
Beneath the Royal Standard,
Blest by our faith in God.
Where would the bees be,
Without their Queen,
Or the ants without their queen, on the hill?
And what would our alternative be,
Would it be by a military regime,
Under the Jack Boot rule,
And their spies, listening for any dissent,
And punishment harsh in a torture cell.
Or would our rule be,
By a Cromwell dictator,
And the downfall, of all that is good.
No, no, give us our freedom,
With our Queen at the helm,
Beneath the Royal Standard,
Of truth and our faith,
In our God.

*B D S Leith*

## THE ROYALS

Let us pay tribute to our lovely Queen,
Who for so many years has graced the scene,
Presiding over many acts of state, and
Gently tending some that might have been.
All through those years, with Philip by her side,
She raised a family, with loving pride,
And then encouraged them along life's road,
Emotionally, with a love that shewed.

Just like her Father, with the common touch,
She came to us - and came to mean so much.
All through the war years, until peacetime came,
Her 'Smiling Duchess' Mother added fame.
Through years of gladness, often tinged with pain,
Shining example, with no thought of gain,
Without the need to raise her voice, or shout.
She taught us what this world is all about.

Long may she reign, elegant in regal state,
Contributing to making Britain Great.
A union of people far and wide,
Supported by her family, at her side,
To reign for many happy years to come,
Beyond the century - to the great millennium!

*Leonard T Coleman*

## THE ROYALS

The Royals have been now
For many a year
Times are changing
Thoughts altering fast
Just how long should the
Royals last?
Their added expense
We could do without
But who would replace
Them? A thought to bear
It isn't that we, the
People, do not care
But times are changing
In every sphere
Are they out dated
In this so-called modern world?
Maybe after the Queen Mother
And our Queen
A new thinking, *should be* seen.

*Joan Patrickson*

## THE ROYALS

They are there and always have been
someone to look up to.
But are they really like that or quite ordinary?
People get excited, when they arrive,
waving flags and shouting
'It's good to be alive.'
There was one Royal above the rest,
we marvel at her name.
She healed the sick with one touch,
a smile, a hug - it meant so much.
Let's hope that we all learnt much from her.
How to reach the people, it's not by roses in the air
and it's so very rare!
It's hands on approach for us,
we really think it's right.
Then we would welcome the Royals,
what a wonderful sight.

*Marion D Harris*

## HRH

Who travels to distant shores,
Studies Arabic tradition,
Wraps her head in a shawl,
Pacifies the war lord,
Prepares ground for diplomats,
Shakes hands with an emperor,
Chats warmly with Mrs Brown,
Happy in a palace,
Happy around town,
Has dustmen up for afternoon tea,
Trains an up and coming king,
Answers for her family,
(Though the blows begin to sting,)
Who, called by duty,
Chose to pay her tax,
Looks to what she promised,
Looks to God and back,
Leads a church,
Leads a nation,
That cries out for her blood,
Does her best,
Though sometimes fails,
She's often passed the test,
Committed to her people,
Undaunted, she's going on,
She can never be perfect,
But for her nation,
*She is strong.*

**Fiona Bower**

## THE ROYALS

You may not believe this, but I am a Royalist at heart,
but I feel that we should rid ourselves of the hangers on, for a start.
There should only be two or three, paid for their work,
the rest should get a job to earn their keep, it wouldn't hurt.
I think that the Queen Mum, is a special case,
she's loved by most people, and at her age she earns her space.
Prince Charles and his sons, they need nothing at all,
as the Duchy of Cornwall's money, is theirs to call.
I think with our Royalty, there is too much bowing and scraping,
after all they are only human, they shouldn't have any special rating.
I'm not communist, but this I strongly believe,
God made us all equal, so no special privileges should any man receive.
I also feel that some of their property, should be sold off for rent,
as it is criminal that so many people are homeless, and the money
would be better spent.

*Ken Mills*

## HRH OR LACK OF

They've taken away my HRH
What a rotten bunch,
Now I'm just a common Duke,
Without a free lunch.

The ladies no longer curtsy,
In their low necked evening gowns,
Showing off their bosoms,
As they swept to the ground.

Men no longer have to bow,
From either neck or waist,
Most could never get it right,
Done in too much haste.

The union flag flies on top of the palace,
It is the end of we Royals,
Royal yacht's already gone,
New Labour's looting all the spoils.

I hope they won't charge me rent,
For my palace in the park,
For if they do I'll have to move,
To Chequers, what a lark.

Will they take my Rolls away,
And offer me a bike?
It appears we have no say,
The new PM just says obey.

Will they sell the Royal regalia,
And shut down the Tower?
Perhaps the Chancellor of the Exchequer
Should live there, his expression is so dour.

But the House of Lords
Will be a sorry sight,
Without the blue bloods
To keep this country right.

*Albert H Williams*

## THE ROYALS

Shall we keep the Royals, or not?
This might put you on the spot.
My decision is quite clear -
Rather than they disappear,
Let's be loyal, and keep the lot!

*Dorothy Campbell*

## DIANA . . .

We wept when we discovered that she'd died -
laid carpets of flowers outside the Palace gates;
wrote endless messages in condolence books;
some hacks expressed regret. Alas, too late.

Criticised in life for opening up her heart,
not keeping a stiff upper lip like the in-laws -
for being too frail to hold it all inside,
in death we saw her power show its claws.

She was flawed, like us all; demanding privacy,
then wooing the media, manipulating
the press when it suited her book, courting attention;
yet her love for the frail was pure, uncalculating.

Her frailty was her strength, and this we loved.
The Windsors were right to fear her, and some saw
that this shy, quiet girl with a hidden spine of steel
would finally destroy the dinosaur.

'I shall not go quietly,' she once openly vowed;
and when she went, she stripped the throne quite bare -
exposing in all its weakness the stiffened heart
of a family born to rule - but not show care.

Yet we all share a part in her untimely death -
demanding to know more about what she might do.
Thus frailty kills the frail. As Wilde wrote:
'And each man kills the thing he loves.' How true.

*J M Service*

## REGAL RUNDOWN

The Queen Mother's the one at the top of the heap
Queen Elizabeth has the crown she's determined to keep
Duke of Edinburgh the patriarch who ruined his sons
Princess Margaret who only chooses the hopeless ones
Prince Charles who tried to follow his mother's rules
Princess Anne despises everyone, not only fools
Prince Andrew who couldn't hold onto his wife
Prince Edward who makes one think 'Please get a life'

*Susan Melville*

## 'SCANDAL?' NEVER!

There has been scandal since way back when
Women were women, and men were men
Affairs of the heart behind closed doors
Were always evident, a chore
British back then were upper crust
Doing things right as of course they must.

No one would tell even if there might -
Be another woman in the Royal house
They would not grouse
Carry on doing what they know best
The people won't let you down, they'll do the rest
That was when England was at its best

Turning a blind eye to the naughty bits
When we the people were all stiff upper lip
Now we're in nineteen ninety eight
There's plenty to whinge about, who knows their fate
I hope they survive, I really do
Without the Royals we loose our heritage too.

So come on Royals sort yourselves out
Let your people know your still about
Hand over the throne to Charles today
Take the lead from your people, hear what they say
Give in gracefully as you should
Give Charles the power, he may do some good!

*Susan Askew*

## DEATH OF A PRINCESS

Like a river they came, pouring, flowing, gathering in pools,
To stand in stunned silence:
And they wept.

Like a scented carpet they lay, symbols of love and loss.
Spreading ever further, candles lighting their way:
Laid by those who wept.

Brightly they burned, in the fragrant air,
Shining beacons of hope, in a world full of despair:
Shrines from those who wept.

Slowly she came, on her long journey home.
Clattering hooves, breaking the silence, bringing the tears:
The policewoman wept.

In their millions they fell, flowing down faces old and young.
Uniting the nation in a tidal wave of grief:
And the world wept.

Packed it was, with Royalty, stars and unknowns,
Paying homage to a princess, taken in full bloom:
And he sang and wept.

So brave they were, walking proudly,
Escorting her home, for the very last time:
Privately they wept.

Alone she is now, covered by a sea of flowers, she sleeps.
Isolated by the adulation, that stirred so much emotion:
No more to pain and weep.

Compelled I watched, as the tragedy unfolded.
Overwhelmed by the sadness of a nation united in mourning:
And I wept.

**Beverley Christian**

## THE ROYALS

Retain pomp and circumstance
As tradition recognisance.
Brings wealth to Britain from overseas,
Tourists eager to watch ceremonies.

Royals are preferable to reign
And their immediate family chain,
Than dictators or presidents
Or any other encumbrance.
But when their kin marry
The onus on Britain we must miscarry;
Except the heir to throne
He or she, spouse and kin alone.

Other descendants and spouse
Should work to maintain themselves and house.
Royal personal antiques and treasures,
Queen needs to take insurance measures.
Not thrust out begging bowl
When property disasters cause large payroll;
Now time to call a halt,
Stress Royals dig deep into their vault.

Necessary figure heads,
We citizens are not dunderheads.
Outer family members expense,
Order be severed, burden dispensed
From Treasury purse.
Head of State should earn subject's respect and worth,
Royal; thro' accident of birth.
Recent fiascos, denials, beyond belief,
They hang perilously from throne by their teeth!

*Hilary Jill Robson*

## ROYALTY PERSONIFIED

Centuries ago, islanders were slaughtered: Invaders stole their land,
Leaving mayhem and injustice, innocent blood on every hand!
Lands and estates were divided, feathered each his own ends.
Kings installed feudal barons; spoils given to their friends.

Serfs and the poor tended feudal land, were crippled with taxes,
The brave who protested, hung and decapitated by axes,
Taking the king's rabbits or game, to feed their family,
No compassion or understanding, just hung from a tree.

Heavier taxes were imposed to raise armies and make war,
Homeless starving widows and orphans, were a legacy of the poor.
Barons and earls wallowed in stolen riches and plundered others'
wealth.
They were opulent, cruel and uncaring, basking in luxury and good
health.

Still living on people's taxation: undeclared private wealth of their own,
Protected by the establishment; secrets never to be known.
No Bill of Rights, Written Constitution, or Freedom of Information Act
here.
Do they really delude this nation, who or what do they fear?

This Ilk have never been friends or protectors of the likes of you and me
Swaggering around in blind arrogance, with eyes that will not see.
Coveted and pampered, by constant 'hangers on'
Believing they are always right; incapable of wrong.

Heads of state, should be chosen and elected by the nation,
Yet they purport to rule, lording over the population.
Democracy should be the right of people, with freedom of choice,
The arrogance of this privileged house, should not have a voice.

The twenty-first century looms loud and clear, to herald Royal demise.
New technology beckons the young; satellite voices from the skies.
Looking back into our history, will show mankind's mistakes of past,
Time for an *elected republic,* inherited privilege replaced at last.

*Jim Wilson*

# RIGHT ROYAL

It makes me angry when I hear people moan
That we have a Queen upon the throne
Yes! and proud we should be
To have a Royal family.
They have things we'll never have it's true
Palaces, treasures, crowns, to name a few.
Because of it people come from around the world
Our history and tradition to see unfurled.
Buckingham Palace, Windsor, Sandringham and more
Visitors come and admire from every shore.
The family itself, just stop and think
They're not always in the pink.
They have their problems too like us
And what happens? The press kick up a fuss.
Their high profile is an extra load
If we have difficulties, no one knows.
Travel round the world and you'll see
People envy us our Royal family.
Other countries where kings and queens reign
Hold their heads high; like Holland and Spain.
That's just a couple, there are several more
Where something lasts, is certain, is sure.
In this fickle changing, material globe
There's something stable in seeing a Royal robe.
Look at sport, art, children and health
Royal talents and work have given a wealth.
I'm sick and tired of new 'cool' Britannia
Our past is our foundation, kick it out! How can ya?
Learn from the past, apply the new, should be the scene
So for me, and I'm not alone, God bless our Queen.

*Jane Uff*

## THANK YOU MA'AM FOR FORTY YEARS

Within sight of Mount Kilimanjaro, so many miles from home,
came a message of great sorrow, and your accession to the throne,
A princess so young and beautiful, and all the world had seen,
your Coronation at the Abbey, as you were crowned our Gracious
                                                                                       Queen.

You are a monarch and a mother, your family now complete,
how your subjects love it, when able to greet you in the street,
The posies they all hand you, tokens of their great esteem,
to a baby known as Lilibet, but now our Gracious Queen.

Your reign has now spanned forty years, sharing our joys and woes,
you are a comfort to the nation, in times of conflict with our foes,
Inspiring your people, a tower of strength is what you've been,
so may we sing for many years; 'God Save Our Gracious Queen'.

***Wenn The Penn***

# THE ROYALS - ONLY HUMAN AFTER ALL!

Queen Elizabeth and Prince Philip, Duke of Edinburgh,
they stand for all that is honourable and upright,
they set a good example for us to follow.

But they are only human,
and cannot pretend to be otherwise.
They brought up four children
and tried to give them all a good start,
but three of them had failed marriages,
although the media may be partly to blame.

Charles and Diana - what a fairytale wedding,
but it certainly wasn't happiness ever after
and they both suffered a lot of pain.

Anne and Captain Mark Phillips,
they may have been lovers of horses,
and they had two lovely children
but their marriage too fell apart.

To say nothing of Andrew and Fergie
- they were both ambitious,
they had two beautiful daughters
but they chose to live apart.

Perhaps Prince Edward, the youngest son,
will meet the perfect match,
and be the one to succeed in
love, marriage and family life.

I'm glad we have a Royal family,
for they do a lot of good.
Let's try harder to support and love them
and give them privacy when they need it.
Remember they are only human after all!

**Cathy Mearman**

## OUR ROYAL FAMILY

Our Queen and Royal family,
Are an institution most respect,
But do they feel the same about us?
For they haven't shown it yet.

That's why when Diana came along,
And showed a more human way,
Most of us learned to love her
And grieved when she went away.

She showed us that we mattered,
She showed us that she cared,
It's all we ask, it's not too much,
I'm sure it can be spared.

If only our Queen would smile more
As if she's enjoying herself,
Instead of giving the impression
She does everything under sufferance,
And then perhaps we'd start to believe
That she likes *us* and cares about *us*.

*D Naylor*

## WHO ASKED US?

So, who asked
them to rule
over us?
Was it you?
Was it me?
Was it God?
Was it all
*three?*

I dunno.

High in their palaces
they do who knows what
while the commoners
in their 2-up and 2-downs
do the only
thing they've
ever known -

trying to survive.

*P J Gassner*

## THIS GRIEF I BEAR

This grief I bear is agonising
As the tears in my eyes are rising.
The tears flow with ease and pain
Whilst upon my bed I am lain.

This grief I cannot bear
I need the love of someone that cares.
Tears are the order of the day
Where is my bright ray?

My ray of sunshine to help me through
For I am in need of rescue.
Yet no panic do I feel
As I wander through this ordeal.

***Denise Shaw***

## ROYAL DELIGHT

If I had been born Royal
Then life would be so sweet;
I'd have the best of everything
And all good things to eat.

I'd never have to go to work
Nor ever catch a bus;
And everyone would fawn on me,
And treat me with such fuss.

And life would be so pleasant
I'd let the years roll by,
And forget about the camel
And the needle's eye.

The rich young ruler's conscience
Need not trouble me,
For I would serve my country,
And myself particularly.

And I'd never think of giving
My fortune to the poor;
For I could smile at them instead,
And still knock at heaven's door.

**L Beardsley**

## THE ROYAL FAMILY

Is it time for the Royal family, to become more low key?
For our country to be run by a president rather than the monarchy
Many feel they cost us money but this isn't completely true
They are our best tourist attraction, creating their own revenue

They make our country special, just like the fairy tales
To have our very own Queen and the Prince of Wales
The much loved Queen Mother, many a Duke or Duchess
The Princess Royal and Diana, whose death caused much distress

Their stately homes are glamorous, a treat for all to see
So many special royal occasions with all the pomp and ceremony
To see the Queen in her horse drawn carriage, wearing her crown
Her velvet cloak edged with ermine over a real silk gown

Living in such leisurely luxury, but really they're busy too
Royal garden parties, state visits and many a charity do
They're always in the limelight, never out of the public eye
Their lives are not their own, right up until the day they die

This family goes back centuries, they are our English history
To many they are worshipped, they have an air of mystery
The troubles within has not helped, their popularity of late
We still should respect the Queen, she is the Head of State.

The press have had a field day, their personal lives they abuse
But whether it be good or bad, they still make front page news
If the nation had to make a decision, if I had to choose
I would vote to keep the monarchy, they'd be too much to lose

*Linda Brown*

## THE ROYALS

I remember thinking back
To the years when I was just a child
Trying to listen to the grown-ups talk
All it seemed to me was a different language
They talked of things, including the Royals
I now realised that they either loved or hated them

As a young adult, I was never really interested
I remember thinking, they were like gods
All of them put on a pedestal
The tabloids just seemed to give them a bad reputation
All they seemed interested in was their wealth
Making people objectionate against them

Just like anything else
We don't like to probe beneath the surface
Because we might just start to like them
And I feel at the end of the day
They're a family, like any other
Wanting the same things as we
To realise our hopes and dreams
Even to feeling desolate, as human beings can feel

Even the dreadful time when Diana died
We were too full of grief and to point the finger
Not acknowledging that they could feel, the same anguish and pain
In society today, they have their individual roles to play
For this country today, for the people
It's time to take them off their pedestal
And start looking beneath the surface
Because we should all have faith

**Lorraine Saunders**

## QUEEN AND COUNTRY

And see the light of England's throne,
Shine as a beacon on the earth,
As setting sun and passing time,
Fail in their quest to dull her realm.

Then as detractors circle near,
So men of England hold their ground,
And in one glorious moment show,
United power in England's crown.

And for this kingdom on the earth,
Is there a price too great to pay,
To keep this nation's heart pounding strong,
And show the Royal Standard high?

Of any symbol of our day,
That brings past victories close to mind,
The light of Windsor's house, of England,
Reflects a glory long to shine.

*Andrew Darkin*

# ROYAL

She was bright and charismatic
Young, graceful, full of charm
Now looks grim and autocratic
'So please to call me Ma'am'

He's got a reputation
For being gruff, unkind
But do you think it was much fun
To walk two steps behind?

Their children all have problems
Heartbreak and stress and strife
But they missed out as youngsters
On normal family life

She was bright and charismatic
Shouldered burdens with no fuss
Perhaps we should remember
It was all done for us.

*Enid Gill*

## NOEL

Xmas comes but once a year,
And for many of us gives joyous cheer,
Love the whisky, or a pint of beer,
So long as it is quite clear.

*Albert Usher*

## TRY TO BE FRIENDLY

When you walk down the street put on a smile
Then people will stop and chat a while
They like to talk about this and that
And most of it is idle chat

It costs nothing to be civil and nice
Or if you do a good deed, expect a price
So learn to be a good citizen
This way you turn into a Christian

Think of the people in your street
Or anyone else you may meet
Try to help them when you can
For that is the way of the Christian

So be a good citizen when you can
It does not matter if woman or man
There could be tears at the end of this
For it could end in marital bliss.

**William Howarth**

## UNTITLED

Alone we strive
To keep our dreams
Alive
Alone we despair
With no one to care
Alone we look out
Onto a winter's
Wonderland
Alone we hope
That someone
Will understand.

***P Allen***

## SUMMERTIME GONE WRONG

It started out as summertime
So warm and nothing moves
But the clouds are grey
And the air has chilled
I can quite expect some snow.

I sit and think of years gone by
With hols to be arranged
Did it still rain then?
Was it miserable?
Or was summertime blue skied?

With trees and flowers all confused
Has nature lost her head?
Would squirrels store?
Or bears hibernate?
I'm sure they're not amused.

Will we see another heat wave?
Where beaches are so packed
Could we rig a tent?
Picnic in the woods?
Can summertime be saved?

**Gillian Connors**

## SPRING

Blue tits in spring
Catch us on their wing!

Birds twittering
As now they sing!

Up and down they fly
Blue, black and white!

After food ever so quick
Guess their venue is lilac!

Yellow chicks too
New bulbs showing through!

Daffs and hyacinth
New slips of mint!

Green leaves unfurling
On the ground, or branches; twirling!

*Marie Barker*

## HEALING HANDS

A broken heart, a shattered mind, a ruined life.
A heart - broken by cruel words.
A mind - shattered by endless pain.
A life - ruined by man's sin. Along the road they lie.
The world comes along.
It touches the heart,
Peers into the mind,
Examines the life - but doesn't ask why.
A man comes along -
He touches the heart,
Looks into the mind,
Examines the life - and then starts to cry.
With healing hands
He binds the heart,
Renews the mind,
Restores the life - then walks on to die.

*Karen Caldwell*

## MOVING ON (WITH GOD)

There are many different phases
Of life that we go through
There's childhood, adolescence,
Middle age - senility too
And each phase brings its problems
Its joys and its pain
It's all a learning process
And we have much to gain
By listening to the Master
The One who knows everything
No other voice is sweeter
For He's the Mighty King
So if we truly trust Him
With our very life
He'll guide and protect us
Throughout all the strife
Then He will enable us
To do His Holy Will
If we'll learn to listen
And also to be still
Still enough to capture
The essence of His love
Which He pours out to us
From His throne above!

*Hilary I Jones*

## Vandals

There's a menacing air in the Close tonight
The vandals are at it again
It isn't a figment
To say we're indignant
Being targeted so now and then.

Hanging baskets have spirited moorings
In the night and all laid upside down
Beside the bright awnings
On velvety lawnings
Rending soft greeny surfaces brown.

Solemn constables scribbled in notebooks
Constant mobiles were barking away
But it hasn't stopped larking
Around the cars parking
Or playing transistors all day.

There are rumours of desperate measures
Giving respite to those who sleep light
So the hard elegante
Have turned vigilante
Secreted in bushes at night.

The leader, we know now, was cautioned
His defences diluted and fraught
Said his mum drank and squandered
While his daddy's mind wandered
With the uppers and downers he'd bought.

So, there's nothing conclusive or settled
All the world is the same, good or ill
We can't blame him too much
Society's such
His condition is our bitter pill.

*Clive W Macdonald*

## DOES AGE MATTER

Does age matter when a person dies?
Does age matter to a child or adult, who cares?
Does time excuse the crime?
Your age is not mine!
What has been done cannot be undone.
But what the final result can be should depend on maturity?
Who will judge and who can say if judgement varies from day to day.
How can 'commit' be changed to remit?
And why should justice be tempered with mercy?
Maybe we search for what is not there,
For if it was the criminals would care.
Without accountability, humanity will always dare.

*Allan Lambert*

## THIS WORLD

This world is full of sadness
Misery and pain.
Some try, to make it better
But, it will always be the same.

All the lands around us,
Are in an awful state,
They don't think of love,
All they can do, 'is hate!'

They want to, 'keep on fighting'
And keep killing too,
Some don't know, 'what they're doing'
They're just like me, and you.

But, we've got to stop, and think.
About the people that will die;
Then we'll 'think and wonder'
For 'whatever' and 'for why?'

*E B Holcombe*

## THE VICTIM

A mugger walked along the street
His eyes upon his prey
I am sure he won't forget
That, *eventful* day

Upon the bench she sat alone
With glasses and white hair
As he lunged for her bag
Her fist flew through the air

She fought, she bit, she scratched, she kicked
She dragged him to the ground
He was starting to regret
This victim, he had found

Into the crowd she disappeared
Breathless from her fight
Then he turned to run away
But something wasn't right

Where had all his money gone
His shoulders he just shrugged
It took some time to accept
That the mugger, had been mugged.

**Dennis N Davies**

## DOES AGE MATTER?

Window smashed to smithereens,
against the wall an old man leans.
Battered, bruised, stunned and shocked,
all the doors securely locked.
Afraid to move . . . his savings gone
he doesn't think he'll last too long.
Neighbours near, they call the law
that's what our police are for.
They'll catch the vandal, there's no doubt,
they'll lock him up, he'll not get out!
Fingerprints taken, thief well-known
he's struck before, they know his home.
His mother screams as cops arrive . . .
She wants her son to stay alive.
He's got a gun . . . she begs . . . 'Don't shoot . . .
he didn't mean to steal the loot,
it's not his fault . . . it's just his gang.'
A voice shouts *'halt,'* a gun goes bang.
A policeman falls, his life snuffed out
at last they catch this evil lout.
He's bundled off to face the court
a lesson now he should be taught.
The judge has heard it all before . . .
he didn't mean to break the law . . .
it's not his fault his dad left home
and there's nowhere but the streets to roam . . .
he's tried so many different schools,
he doesn't mean to break the rules.
He'll *never* steal or kill again . . .
they let him go . . . he's only ten!

*J L Thorne*

## RETURN TO MORAL VALUES

'String them up, lock up their parents,' is the universal cry,
But there'll always be bad apples, no matter what we try.
There are greedy youngsters, where enough is never enough,
Youngsters join older youths in gangs to prove that they are tough.

While most parents and teachers, try to teach what's right from wrong,
Seems that society's morals have collapsed and gone.
We must get back to basics, manners, politeness too,
Passing on moral values makes life good for me and you.

*Susan Mullinger*

# AGELESS

Sat over the street gutter, abused guts heaving,
head in hands confusion whirls beyond relieving,
discarded her shoes for the cold putrid paving
as scant clothing crumples with skeletal raving.
Her stale mouth swears fresh allegiance to a teetotal way
her addiction lies easy, it will all times hold sway;
a veteran of the pub crawl, party pass-outs, forgotten nights,
she's stood on the sidelines of innumerable drunken fights.
Dead eyes see frosted tarmac reaching for her face
while kaleidoscopic features of friends amusement and disgrace
crowd the ill-lit gaps of her pulsating vision,
as paralysis moulds her to the curb in numbing fusion.
Yellow skin quakes, as she 'spews' once again
sour liquid falls to the dark soulless drain,
she desires nothing more than to be left there to die
for the slightest of movements makes her abdomen cry
again comes the rumbling from deep in her girth
and panic assists in the dread of cold earth
piled freely above her as black-gowned friends turn to go,
when, could they but hear her, then they might know
she felt she was living, as she raced life away,
the night-life, unremembered, kept reality at bay.
left feeling like fifty, she's but fifteen . . . about,
and the inebriated nightmare? It's just simply passed out.

*M C Lawrence*

## FREEDOM?

What does freedom mean to you? Does it mean to say and do,
Anything that strikes your brain, though it causes others pain?
The sort of game that has no rules, is one that's only played by fools.
I often hear the view today, that the out of work who get no pay,
should be excused, if time to time, because they're poor,
have turned to crime,
who when depressed, become depraved, destroying things,
for which we've saved,
stealing cars, and pushing drugs, to me they're nothing more than thugs.

I too, knew hunger in earlier years, as did many of my peers.
We'd no desire to destroy, a neighbour's treasured pride and joy,
because it was beyond our reach, a lesson this age fails to teach.
Our parents' moral guidance, I'm pleased and proud to say,
brought the pride in our behaviour, so seldom seen today.
The so-called freedom most sought today it sadly seems to me,
is neither from poverty nor persecution, but responsibility.

*Ray Baker*

## CHILDREN OF DELINQUENCY

Nothing to do nothing to say
Their lives are filled with idle play
First glue then weed then the harder stuff
Reality is not enough.

They're never here they're always there
For place and time they do not care
They take they burn it's all for show
Their minds are seeds that will not grow.

We say that they should act their age
But to act you need a stage
Society must take the blame
And teach them how to play the game.

And maybe someday we will tame
The children of delinquency.

**Carl A Dignan**

## QUESTIONS

What should Mother and Father do
to keep their loved ones in check?
There are laws in place
to prevent the wringing of a neck.

Should they be sent to their room
be admonished for ever more?
If they disobey in their room
should they follow and lock the door?

All sorts of advice is given
many of conflicting views,
how to bring your children up
to prevent them from being 'news'.

What an amazing race we are
we love to hand advice around,
though when it is given to us
we often become very profound.

What are we to act upon
what appears on our TV screen?
When is your child an adult
are there children, say, of nineteen?

*Trevor Vincent*

## WHERE THE FAULT LIES

To a child it's just a game
They're all the same,
Seeing adults engaged in crime
On TV and video all the time.
Naturally they will imitate
And if parents come home too late
To switch off the more violent scenes
That dominate our late-night screens,
Only then does the child go to bed
With violence and crime filling its head -
So now, the die is cast,
But prison must be the very last
On our list of punishments,
Board them instead in educational establishments
Where they can see, and feel love,
Have role models far above
Those they had in the past.
This would produce a cure to last
A lifetime for each child's body, spirit and mind,
To face the future, let the shadows fall behind -
But let those who are at fault
Pay the boarding fees -
  To right the wrong that they have wrought.

*Thomas C Ryemarsh*

## NOT A BIT

Baby longed for, loved by all
Becomes nurtured child, succeeds at school.
Baby unwanted, ignored by all
Becomes unloved child, rebels, that's cool?
Nurtured child, gently but firmly guided
Never strays, when loyalties become divided.
Unloved child, nobody's little treasure,
Can one really find a measure
To gauge the damage already unfurled?
Is it any wonder, he rejects the world
To thieve, bully, violate?
Knows no love, so why not hate?
The rest of us don't care too much
So, sorry kid, you are out of luck.
Go to prison, do your time
Learn more tricks down the line.
Does age matter? Not a bit,
You are bad, bad, bad and
Just turned six!

*Vivienne Doncaster*

## MYSTERY OF MURDER

We are left with the image of a young child,
He's lying face down in a shallow puddle,
His grieving mother is surrounded by photographs
and mourns for the son she yearns to cuddle.
His killer was not condemned by trial or jury,
There was never a question that he'd serve time,
He was only a boy aged three
and unaware that he'd committed such a crime.
It was a tantrum that turned into a tragedy
although it left behind a trail of victims,
All of them search for a reasonable explanation
and as for the boy, what will become of him?
Age does matter when there are tragic consequences
but in this case a prison cell would not do,
Justice will come in time when he has realised
the suffering he put both families through.
As for blame, who do we point the finger at?
Society, lack of control or something he had seen,
If we could understand or make sense of it all,
We may have prevented crimes that have already been.

*Kathleen Speed*

## INFECTED YOUTH
## A CRIMINAL GENE

Little education, no discipline,
What kind of society are we living in,
Where children are criminals, the culprits of crime,
Unlike the youth of previous times.
The fault of the parents, no, who is to blame,
A bad generation, the newspapers claim.
Is it correct to throw them in jail,
Is it their fault or has society failed?
So what can we do but face up to the truth?
The criminal gene has infected our youth.

***Samantha Mitchell***

## AND SO TO BED

The crack of log in inglebook
Fingered cover of favourite book
A loving look, a glass of wine
The drapes are drawn. Our world is fine.
We simple folk ask less of life
What joy there is in a loving wife
She tends the house with so much care
And cooks my meals of country fare
My clothes are clean and smell so sweet
And she herself so trim and neat.
With shining hair tied in a bun
Her twinkling eyes so full of fun
Slim fingers push a fallen lock
From off my brow, while we take stock
Of worldly matters, which we discuss
Deciding not to make a fuss.
We've toiled so hard for a long, long time
Now life has eased and it's quite sublime.
I take her hand and lead her on
Towards the stairs at set of sun.
A fond embrace, and a loving kiss
These things we need to make life bliss.

*Carrington Lee*

## APOLOGY

You cannot trust the lads at seventeen to twenty
They mean it when they say it
But their brain box is still quite empty.
It takes a further year or two, sometimes a living age
For boys becoming men to see the error of their ways.
It isn't spite or selfishness
It isn't simply 'Couldn't care less'
It's just because a boy is a lad.
He is not the dad the lass would have.

Though pregnant and with child she may
Consider why that boy would betray her love
To let her down and be so cold
As not to see her in her distress
Don't think that he just 'Couldn't care less'
Lads dream on and on, memories fade in the mist
It's only later when they're older and they reminisce
How stupid. What a fool I was, and all because, and all because
If only. Why didn't I, I really wish I had
But then, he really was. *Just a little lad.*

**Roy Brown**

## SECOND WIND

Faster Dandad faster
as my knees hit the floor with a thump
while tiny boots, were kicking my ears
a small hand was slapping my rump.

At breakneck speed we galloped
round the kitchen, and out through the hall
and who would think that at sixty-five
one could move very fast at all.

then the wife said, think of your age dear
so I looked up at her, and I grinned
but damn it all, I'm having a ball
and I'm just getting my second wind.

Now some people are born, to be wealthy
while others strive to be fit
but I'm the luckiest man of all
with a grandson who's two and a bit.

*Roy Turke*

## DOES AGE MATTER?

My mother told me that when I was aged between two and ten
I was always asking; what, why, who, which, where and when?

When I was learning, grasping knowledge, between ten and twenty
The questions I asked were awkward, blush-making, and plenty.

Between twenty and thirty
My thoughts were quite dirty

From thirty to forty
My thoughts were naughty

From forty to fifty
I became much less nifty

From fifty to sixty
I drank too much whisky

From sixty to seventy
Life wasn't heavenly

From seventy to eighty
I'd grown overweighty

By the time I reach ninety
I think I just mightn't be!

*Joan Scowcroft*

## DOWN

Stone-grey beard on an ash pale face,
Deep furrowed lines, cracked like lace.
Fingers yellow from tobacco stain,
Shabby shoes still wet from rain.
A worn thin coat, trousers held with twine,
Tight in his hand, cheap red wine.
No place to sleep it is a shame,
What caused this? Is he to blame?

*J R Wiseman*

## MOTHER LOVE

The sweetest person you ever met
That's why in my life I'll never forget
Though she is gone now thirty years
And time has dried up all the tears

She's always in my thoughts and dreams
She's with me always so it seems
And with me still in memory's haze
Still showing her love in many ways

Be kind to your mum I now advise
To be good and honest and tell no lies
You'll find her the best friend you've ever had
She'll always love you, her bonny wee lad.

*S T Jennings*

## THE AGED AND OUR YOUNG

Sometimes loud, sometimes brash
to our frailty. At other times kind,
outgrowing fast our gradual retreat
of body and mind.

The young of our sons and daughters,
rather special although not elite, with
an age gap betwixt and between.
Alas, if our lives do not meet.

The future of our country, as our
Queen says, 'Is in their hands' being
flesh of our flesh they feel pain,
like those who once saved our land.

They need our caring love for them,
enough to help cope with their dreams.
Not be selfish and turn away from them,
when we do not always agree.

Making life a better example,
turning dross into ways that are good.
With tolerance and patience to show them,
if only the strong people would.

Our Lord forgave all our weakness
with love and humility, to overcome
all barriers as the wise will often
perceive.

To become the perfect 'example'
their love reaching full and free,
open to all, in acceptance
for 'people' whoever they be.

*Phoebe J Laing*

# HAND IT TO ME ON A PLATE

They say age doesn't matter
Well, I beg to differ, you see
Wine whisky and women
Are much better with maturity

I'm baking a cake today
It took years and years to cook
Here are the ingredients
Would you like to take a look?

Take an extra large spoonful
Of the experience of life
Mix carefully with smiles and sorrow
And a pinch of strain and strife

Throw in a little wisdom
Then bake and see it rise
The result will be maturity
You can see it in my eyes

In earlier years I was offered pudding
The desert was called 'Quick, give it to me'
Needed was a bank book
A few poppers and a soft mammy

Mixed with it was stubbornness
And the selfishness of 'me, me, me'
It was a rich pudding
It was the pudding of delinquency

Now I never bother with the pudding
It sounds rather nasty to me
I'll settle for a slice of the cake
The cake of maturity.

*Maureen Albert*

## Time For Spring

Strong cold winds cause leaves to fall
Sometimes heaps them up by the garden wall,
Or leaves them untidy on the ground.
Often amongst them berries and nuts can be found,
Or put into compost heaps to decay,
Or put in bags to be thrown away.
Into hedges some will go
To be covered by frost or snow.
A hedgehog would collect the best,
To make a warm home for it to rest.
Only the holly and yew stand proud,
The holly may be cut by a crowd.
Small evergreens could be a Christmas tree,
Potted and decorated for all to see.
Now cold high winds really blow,
Soon be winter and it could snow.
When you hear the robin sing,
You will know it's time for spring.

*Margaret Upson*

## THE SWAYING ROWAN TREE

Oh! Lovely swaying Rowan Tree
I'm glad you are in my garden,
Near to the road where all can see
Your branches like tapers fluttering.
The breeze blows soft through little leaves
Then, when the month of May arrives
Sweet and white-flowered bunches
Hang there to show just how you thrive,
And, every year, it seems quite clear
Your mission to life was shaped
By the 'Great One' on High, so dear
Would place on you, the happy task
Late autumn feeding the birds who grasp
Branches there for sustenance so sweet.
Yes, the clusters of red berries,
They love to come and feast in droves
To collect their lovely treasure trove.
Now autumn is here, lovely Rowan Tree
Leaves leaving you on the wind.
Yet, gracefully year by year alive
The birds come to you, like bees to a hive.

*Pearl Mansell*

## An Everlasting Spring Day

Willow trees blowing with a cool, slight breeze
Soft green grass blustering this way and that
Ash-grey squirrels bounding over the rooftops
Slinking along the white wall slopes a velvet black cat
Poppies poking out their ruffled, scarlet petals
Filling the clean air with a sweet, heathery scent
Crickets chirping together in perfect harmony
'O what a heavenly morn we have been sent!'
Pigeons in flocks flying through the sea-blue sky
Swarms of bees going about their busybody way
Slithering worms peeking their heads out like never before
'O 'tis a wonderful, glorious fine spring day!'
Carpets of colourful flowers spread before me
Swinging their heads gaily from side to side
Merry little children skipping along together
With a playful, cuddly puppy as their furry guide!
As the content time keeps on rolling by
Everyone retires home for a well-deserved rest
Of all the four seasons, all year round
I certainly know which one I like best!

Tick-tock, the grandfather clock is awakening everyone
Announcing that another spring day has just begun.

*Malaka Chowdhury*

## SPRING

Spring is showery, flowery, bowery,
I love the way spring feels,
The lovely cool wind rubbing against my face,
And the way it showers upon the fields,
The colourful flowers with watery pearls,
And flowers with little curls,
Pink, yellow, blue, purple all the colours are mixed.
This world has even a flower with a colour of six,
The lovely showering with a bit of sun,
The rainbow that appears
In the spring season,
There is only one fun of the rainbow, we know,
And the lovely thing around us that glows,
And the little birds that sit upon the crows!

***Fatima Jamshad (16)***

# KALEIDOSCOPE

Spring is the season of renewal and rebirth,
As all nature awakens, replenishing the earth -
Daffodils, crocuses and sprays of blossom appear,
Farmers plant wheat and barley, as lengthening days endear,
And, in greening fields lambs play, as many sweet songs are sung
By the newly arrived birds, building nests for their young.

Then hot summer brings glorious long, sunny days,
The roses in full bloom, with bright colour ablaze;
Butterflies and buzzing bees vie for space in the air,
As, with T-shirts, shorts and swimwear, families prepare,
Both at home and abroad, to fulfil holiday dreams -
A mix of basking in the sun with cooling swims and ice creams.

Autumn turns the leaves russet, gold, yellow and brown,
Before being stripped from the trees to instead carpet the ground;
Hibernating animals prepare for long months of sleep,
Gathering winter store, in the ground to bury deep;
And their long journey south the migrant birds will begin,
As fruit-laden branches are emptied, and the harvest gathered in.

Winter brings short, chilly days, the nights long and dark,
The now bare branches of trees appearing lifeless and stark;
It blankets whole landscapes in purest white virgin snow,
To children's exhilaration, their faces aglow;
And we don warm coats, gloves and scarves to shield from icy blasts,
As birds search for crumbs and berries, to survive whilst winter lasts.

Each season has a beauty, texture and mood of its own,
With its own unique wardrobe and melodious tone,
Yet all blending together inextricably
To show a rich kaleidoscope of divine tapestry;
And gazing with awe at Mother Nature's ever-changing display
We praise Almighty God for so ordering things this way

*Ian Caughey*

## AUTUMN LEAVES

Autumn leaves brush my feet -
The smell of autumn; so full, so sweet,
Autumn leaves fall to the ground
Not a whisper, not a sound.

An acorn falls from a tree:
An oak tree knowing it will be.
The acorns falling, fast, asleep . . .
Awakens: spring, when snowdrops weep.

When I see snowdrops on the ground,
Snowy-white, snow all around -
A teardrop falls, so profound . . .
Not a whisper, not a sound.

**Michael A Moore**

## The Changing Seasons

Spring is a wonderful season the earth comes to life
Seedlings grow, plants and flowers reach for the light
Gardens are tilled, farmers work hard in the fields
Earth rewards us for toil we put in, to reap a good yield,
Baby lambs are born, birds sing in the trees
Primroses grow, daffodils sway gently in the warm breeze.

Summer is my favourite time, I love the warmth of the sun
With clear blue sky overhead, and no dark clouds around,
Masses of flowers in full bloom in parklands and in gardens
Sun sparkling on a river winding between ferns and bracken
It's great to walk along the beach breathing in the salty air
And watch the waves rolling in and splashing against the pier.

Autumn is time for harvesting, and gathering in the hay
The fruits of the earth are blessed as we kneel in church and pray.
Autumn is like a rainbow, full of glorious colour
As green leaves turn to copper, it makes you stop and wonder
How nature changes each season in such a special way
After vivid leaves float to the ground they gradually fade away.

Winter means dark dreary days, coughs and colds
With bitter winds, rain, hail, and snow.
Not my favourite season, it's much too cold and stormy,
Thunder, lightning, and gale force winds rattle down the chimney.
Branches of trees stripped bare, everywhere is bleak,
Frost is white upon the ground, and hard beneath my feet.

*Lorna June Burdon*

## AUTUMN DAYS

The mellow days of autumn bring
Contentment. After harvesting
Silos are full of golden corn.
Now hop fields lie naked, forlorn
Because surrounding poplar trees
Shed yellow leaves in autumn breeze.

The farmer drives to stubbled field;
Plough behind tractor . . . heavy wheeled
To cope with stony, damp, clay ground.
Eager gulls watch where he is bound.
Noisily they wheel, dip and rise
Against the mellow autumn skies.

He turns into a waiting field
And as he ploughs . . . the soil will yield
A harvest of another kind.
The hungry gulls now land behind
The plough and feast on insect fare
Before the field lies cold and bare.

Proud trees now dressed in golden gowns;
Others in bronze or blushing browns
Release their leaves which skip and prance
In gay confusion as they dance
Along the ground. Then Nature weaves
An autumn carpet of dead leaves.

As autumn days come to an end
Luke's little summer comes to spend
Seven warm days of sunshine bright;
So autumn colours can delight
Our eyes and hearts. Now short'ning days
Remind us winter's on the way.

*Elwynne*

## Autumn

Wild wind roaring in chimney flue
Sets a scene of autumnal gloom,
Windswept clouds with breaks of blue
Are swiftly swept by nature's broom.

Migrant songsters now long-gone
To a warmer sunnier clime
With the memory of their song
Fades like the sands of time.

Grey mist enshrouding the rolling hills
Seems to reach up to the sky,
All rhythm of life slows and stills
And curling leaves abandoned lie.

In hope new buds already form
To brave cold winter's might
Defiant of the autumn's storm
To greet the springtime bright!

*B Wilson*

## AUTUMN LEAVES

What a wonderful sight to behold
The falling leaves of red, green, yellow and gold.
They are everywhere, all around,
Like a multicoloured carpet, covering the ground.
The sun has begun to wane now,
Its heat almost gone.
The last rose of summer,
Spiders' webs with the dew on.
A little robin sings his heart out,
Jenny wren searching for food,
What a time of the year, this is,
It puts you in a great mood.
The leaves that rustle underfoot,
Conkers all shiny and brown,
Chestnuts, not quite ready,
But the wind's blown some of them down.
Do we appreciate our seasons,
Are we all aware,
What a miserable land
Our land would be
With everything barren and bare?

*S Buckingham*

## WINTER CHEER

Flakes float gently down outside,
Now it is time to decide,
Do I stay in with the warm winter cheer,
Watching the telly with a glass of beer,
Put my feet up, look at the tree,
Cheese and biscuits, a cup of tea,
Christmas cards, cheerful and merry,
A Christmas pud with a cherry,
Presents to open, presents to enjoy,
Watch their faces with pride and joy?
Or do I become a child,
And go completely wild.
Go out in the cold outside,
Sit in the sledge for a downhill ride,
Play with the white, white snow,
Hear Santa's bell ringing, *ho, ho, ho!*
Dress up warmly, scarf, gloves, hat,
Have a snowball fight - *splat!*
Build a snowman, twigs, leaves, stones,
Roll around so much I bruise my bones?
Which one snow or beer?
Go for both it's the winter cheer!

*Jessica Street*

## WHEN WINTRY WINDS BLOW

Amongst my favourite things
are a snowy blanket and wintry winds.
The earth looks peacefully asleep
under the frosty snow so deep.
Snowflakes swirl in the light morning breeze
falling from the sky with undisguised ease,
drifting along while the winter wind blows.
How long it will last . . . nobody knows.
The wintry wind has branches torn . . .
off the trees standing empty and forlorn.
The wind has drifted the snow low and high.
To shift that lot, you can but try!
Glistening frosty in the moonlight
the countryside looks a beautiful sight.
Squirrels and birds . . . no doubt . . . are sheltering
till the wind stops and snow is melting.
The wintry winds seem to have a spell
over people . . . and animals as well.
Cows and sheep are coated in an extra layer of white,
transformed into ghosts by wind and frost during the night;
but when the sun shines, again, bright,
everywhere sparkles with a new light.

*Annemarie Poole*

## AUTUMN WHISPERS

Autumn whispers 'Time to be gone'
'My turn now, I am the one'
Summer sunshine, gentle breezes,
Holidays, ladybirds, everything pleases

Now leaves twirling gracefully, russet parade
Geese drifting southwards, grey cavalcade
Clip clop of horses, day's work done,
Jed looks to farmer, ready for fun.

Wait now for bonfire, spiralling smoke,
Perhaps heavy rainfall, be ready for soak.
Children collect conkers, as we did of yore,
Some things don't change, just memories in store.

But whether it's spring with daffodils yellow,
Cloudless blue sky, followed pale sunset mellow,
Winter with storms, but warm cosy fire,
Autumn, monarch majestic, supreme now, as season's desire.

**Grace Wade**

## AUTUMN FALLS

Autumn dawns and with it the demise of summer and song,
Tired and weary from those hot long nights,
Its soft breeze cools and calms the spirit with its beautiful sights,
Crisp leaves falling gently covering the ground,
Trees and shrubs starting to shed as we merge in the sound,
The autumn falls so as to show,
Just like all living things we have to change and grow,
Not afraid, or to care,
Seasons and changes are intricate parts of living,
Oh autumn we welcome you as you show us our goals,
Paving the way for winter, rejuvenating our souls . . .

*Peggy Keogh*

## WINTER

There is a dark threat in every cloud
Is it cold? Is it fear? Nature shivers
As winter slowly spreads its icy shroud
Extinguishing estival colours

Is it cold? Is it fear? Nature shivers
Winter keeps breathing its damp cold air
Extinguishing estival colours
Trees get undressed till they stand bare

Winter keeps breathing its damp cold air
Insects in their cosy cocoons hide
Trees get undressed till they stand bare
Trying to survive the wintry tide

Insects in their cosy cocoons hide
Birds seek refuge in their own silence
Trying to survive the wintry tide
Life slips into sleepy indolence

Birds seek refuge in their own silence
Each year it's more or less the same
Life slips into sleepy indolence
Nature feels neither guilt nor shame

Each year it's more or less the same
There is a dark threat in every cloud
Nature feels neither guilt nor shame
As winter slowly spreads its icy shroud

**J-C Chandenier**

## Changing Seasons

'How I'd love to live in Spain
Only sunshine no more rain!'
This refrain is often heard
But for me it's just absurd.

The sun's alright - just now and then
Not constant - that's for 'foreign' men
Our climate is so mild and fine
The seasons changing - just divine.

The winter evenings spent inside
With fireside glowing - there we hide
Like hibernating mammals all
'Til springtime beckons with its thaw.

The trees start leafing, buds are seen
The countryside is lush and green
Like waking from a slothful sleep
Yearly metamorphosis keep.

Yes - sunshine's fine - just now and then
Like filling glasses - please say when
To switch it off when it's too hot
For you it's fine, for me it's not.

*Sonia Richards*

## A Whole Year

I cannot decide no matter how I try,
To choose a season, a part of a year, but why.
Why would I choose, when all holds
their own special place in time.

Like spring, when everything awakes.
When young things live and breath.
When flowers grow, and trees
begin to cover themselves in leaves.

Summer, a time to laze,
to reflect on times gone before.
The heat of the blazing sun
suspended in bright blue skies, and more.
People are happier, friendlier and smile.
They say hello, stop and chat for a while.

Autumn, chilly days with that special feel.
Hazy sunshine in crispier skies, a strange appeal.
Wildlife prepare for winter to come,
making nests to keep themselves warm.
Trees shed their leaves, which carpet the ground
in beautiful shades of red, gold and brown.

Winter, with dark days and black nights.
Roaring fires, houses with welcoming lights.
A beautiful sight as snowflakes fall.
In early morn, a footprint is found,
of some small animal searching around,
whilst others have hibernated under the ground.

All these seasons cannot compare.
They all contribute to make a whole year.

*Susan J MacDonald*

## NATURE'S DIARY

Spring, a time of year,
When nature wakes her child,
Sleepy snowdrops raise their heads,
New-born lambs run wild.

Summer brings the long hot days,
Colour carpets the land,
Man seeks solace from their toil,
Children sculpture the sand.

Autumn brings a wondrous scene,
Gold festoons the trees,
Nature's feeling sleepy now,
As a chill envelops the breeze.

Winter comes and log fires burn,
Landscape painted white,
God's small creatures rest their heads,
And nature says goodnight.

*R R Shepherd*

## SPRINGTIME
*(To my younger son)*

My heart aches so again
Something to do with this time of year.
You were born, and the daff's were blooming
And, later your pleasure in them
When a little boy
And for the second time I was
So very happy with two sons
And the happy times that followed,
Especially over the next few years
When you needed us,
I didn't think of
 it ever ending.

***Sheila M Tebbutt***

## THE ROSE TREE THAT GREW AGAIN

The rose tree in our garden
It seemed had had its day
It had been there for many years
That much I've got to say
No roses in their beauty
Had blossomed forth or bloomed,
And all in all the rose tree
Looked withered up and doomed.

And so the only thing to do,
Was to cut the old tree down,
And then to buy another one
Next time we went to town.
So this my husband did for me
And threw the tree away
And then we thought no more of it,
Until a future day.

When we returned from holiday
We found to our delight
The first stalk of a new tree
Already was in sight.
The roots could not be got at,
Deep in the ground they lay,
And now my new rose tree to all,
I'm able to display.

*Irene Dodd*

## AUTUMN PRAYER

Another yearly cycle nears fulfillment,
but nature shows no fear of its future,
of the short death of winter.
Its ageing face glows
with glory, not with despondency.
Beauty which is alien
to the budding of spring
and the vitality of summer
rushes forth in a multitude of colours.
Shades of reds, oranges and yellows
relish with gladness
the coming, necessary sleep of winter,
so that its rebirth in spring may follow.

When the autumn of my life arrives,
may I be like nature, and welcome it
in glory, not with despondency.
May my personality become more colourful,
more varied in its shades;
may my temperament become more beautiful,
with new virtues bursting forth;
and may I relish with gladness
the coming, necessary winter of sleep
knowing that when I awake it will be
during another spring of my rebirth.

**David Rhine**

## SEASONS CHANGE

Golden leaves on treetops green
Bow their heads to autumn's scene

Shades of green from light to dark
Leave trees standing, naked . . . stark!

Branches hang their lifeless limbs,
Resting, until the springtime sings.

Winter now looks grey and dim,
As hungry ducks . . . across the icy lakes skim.

Summer clouds turn to rumbling grey,
Blocking out the summer's rays.

Some seasons come like gentle rain,
Others come, as speeding trains.

Seasons come, and then they go,
All come as friends . . . never foe!

*Sylvia Connor*

# SUBMISSIONS INVITED
## *SOMETHING FOR EVERYONE*

**ANCHOR BOOKS '99** - Any subject, light-hearted clean fun, nothing unprintable please.

**WOMENSWORDS '99** - Strictly women, have your say the female way!

**STRONGWORDS '99** - Warning! Age restriction, must be between 16-24, opinionated and have strong views. (Not for the faint-hearted)

All poems no longer than 30 lines.
Always welcome! No fee!
Cash Prizes to be won!

Mark your envelope (eg *Poetry Now*) *'99*
Send to:
Forward Press Ltd
1-2 Wainman Road, Woodston,
Peterborough, PE2 7BU

**OVER £10,000 POETRY PRIZES
TO BE WON!**

Judging will take place in October 1999